Prairie Smoke

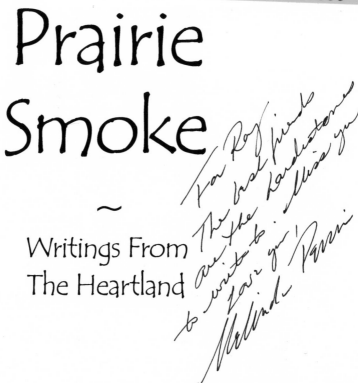

~

Writings From
The Heartland

Melinda Morris Perrin

Ice Cube Press
North Liberty, Iowa

Prairie Smoke: Writings From the Heartland

© 2005 Melinda Morris Perrin

First Edition

Ice Cube Press
205 N Front
North Liberty, Iowa
52317-9302
319/626-2055
www.icecubepress.com

ISBN 1-888160-10-1

Library of Congress Control Number: 2004107869

The paper used in this publication meets the minimum requirements of the American National Standard for Information Sciences—Permanence of Paper for Printed Library Materials, ANSI Z39.48-1992

Manufactured in the United States of America

Cover photos © Melinda Morris Perrin

Dedicated
to
Danny

Thank you to all who opened my eyes, my ears, and my heart and who taught me to appreciate the beauty of the land and the simple gifts of plants, friendship, love, and truth. I am grateful and in return offer these writings in trust that others may receive your gifts through me.

In memory of:
Jim Gillihan
Marilla Missbach
Linda Joan Hodes
Ray Schulenberg
Joe Schumacher
Nakomis Keewaydinoquay
Grandfather Grey Wolf

Two decades of life in the Midwest left me with wonderful memories and these poems. All were written in my time there, with one exception: "The Hawk Blew in from Chicago Last Night" was written a month after we moved back to upstate New York, when I realized how much of the Midwest I had brought with me.

Table of Contents

Earth Renewal Invocation

SOUTH…Teach us to love the Earth,
That we may live in harmony with it.

WEST…Teach us to love ourselves,
That we may learn to help the Earth.

NORTH…Teach us to love one another,
That there may be peace on the Earth.

EAST…Teach us to see the pattern,
That we may know that we are all connected.

April 1994

The Seasons

Spring is a Temptress

Spring is a temptress who teases us with warm gentle breezes,
then turns a cold shoulder.
Her achingly soft colors lie on beds stark with greys and blacks.
Her promise is in the pregnant fingertips of trees
and the tender shoots pushing up from rain-softened earth.
Her siren song lures birds from their sojourn south,
and their voices combine, persuading the sun to come early and
      stay late.

Child-woman, she skips across the waters,
pushing the lamb soft clouds high above.
Her power is new found and fickle.
She awakens the animals from slumber, forgetting their hunger.
She coaxes the purple crocus to show its glory through a blanket
      of snow.
But like our first love, she is first in our hearts and we forgive her.
Our pulse quickens at first sight of her.
for she reminds us that we too were once young.
Spring is a temptress who teases us with warm gentle breezes.

April 15, 1993

Summer Magic

With a dramatic gesture, Summer drapes her mantle of green cross
      the land
And the Earth is reborn.
She dips her sun-touched body into the waters, warming them.
Her golden hair adds sparkles to their surface.
The animals come down to waters' edge to drink in her beauty.
Slowly she rises from her swim,
Water falling as gentle rain from her round, full form.
She walks across fields and meadows, dripping magic.
Flowers turn to seed and seed becomes fruit, ripe and lush,
All from the touch of Summer.
She is love. She is passion. We look forward to each day she brings.
With a dramatic gesture, Summer drapes her mantle of green cross
      the land
And the Earth is reborn.

April 21, 1993

Autumn is a Warrior

Autumn comes with his gaudy many-colored cloak,
bright and brash against a brilliant blue sky.
He lounges among the rolling hills soaking in the lengthening
       rays of the sun,
then rides with vigor in the moonlit night, falling leaves swirling
       in his wake.
His body, lean and hard, is brown with the days of summer sun.
His swaggering stride full of confidence and power.
His laughter rolls like thunder through the valley.

Autumn is a warrior doing battle against the growing dark.
His days are numbered, marked by leaves falling like pages from a
       calendar.
But he lives them to the fullest, scorning those who mourn their
       passing.
He deserves a hero's welcome.
He deserves a hero's glory.
He is the best of what is in us.
Autumn comes with his many-colored cloak,
Bright and brash against a brilliant blue sky.

April 15, 1993

Winter Song

Tall and straight and unyielding, Winter comes to cleanse the Earth.
His regal procession is heralded softly.
First a few delicate snowflakes fall from the palest of grey skies.
A thin sheet of ice is seen on the pond in the early morning light.
Animals sniff the air catching his scent, then hurry to get ready.
Squirrel scurries to hide a few more seeds.
Rabbit's fur turns white with fear.
Bear lumbers down from the high country to slumber in a cozy cave.
Soon the waters are frozen hard.
Tree's bare branches bend against the icy blast of Winter's song.
The world seeks protection under a blanket of snow, but
Tall and straight and unyielding, Winter comes to cleanse the Earth.

April 23. 1993

Spring is a Triumph

Spring was on time, but I was late,
Late in clearing winter's debris.
The crocuses had fought their way
Without my aid or encouragement.
Decked in purple, stripes, and gold,
They looked like a royal entourage.
Gently I broke apart last season's blanket,
Freeing the flowers to follow the sun.

Hungry for more, I searched for signs
Of favorite perennials early return.
Each new revelation lifted my heart.
Each was a triumph, a renewal of life.
Purple shoots of baby Mint lay close to the earth,
Dwarfed for now by the unfolding ears of wild Ginger.
Pointy-hard stalks of Lily of the Valley were encroaching
On the gentle yet tenacious Violets.
Spring bulbs were already well on their way:
Hyacinths, Narcissus, Tulips and all.
Peony's dark rose shoots were almost as tall.

But where were my Evening Primroses?
My carefully transplanted friends from back home?
They had followed me everywhere,
In each little place that we called our own.
Each year I noticed, they migrated a little,
Carried on Chicago's persistent winds.
Each year fewer returned,
Rather like children who've grown and flown.
Then I found them. Their little rosettes
Huddled under dry papery leaves.
Tears filled my eyes; they hadn't deserted,

But moved their colony to less pressured space!
As I tended my small backyard garden,
I was touched to discover how much they all meant.
I welcomed each flower, each herb, and each friend
For each was a triumph, a renewal of life.

April 1996

Summer Makes Me Itch

Sitting on the summer grasses
Red criss-cross welts upon my legs
Green grass stains upon my seat.
It smells so good, and then I sneeze.
Summer makes me itch.

Flying insects hum round my ears,
I bat at them and nervously rub my skin.
Their bites draw blood and are a bother,
I scratch; they itch. Yep,
Summer makes me itch.

Walking through the woods
Raspberry prickles scrape my skin.
Welts form, bumps come.
I hate it when
Summer makes me itch.

Heat's the worst, and then humidity.
Together they make me sweaty and prickly.
Salty rivulets crease my neck.
They irritate and once again,
Summer makes me itch.

Winter's skin is dry and flaky.
Spring's moisture brings a brief respite.
Autumn's glow fades soon enough, but
Summer…
Summer makes me itch.

June 20, 1996

Bittersweet

Bittersweet is the gift of Autumn.
The blazing-forth of the hard berry,
Bright against twisted, dried stalks.

Bittersweet holds bitter-truth,
All the more poignant
Against the certainty of coming snows.

Its orange a brilliant blend.
Yellow for the love within the heart,
Red for the fire, which burns hottest
Before it's extinguished forever.

Framed in stiff, dried petals,
Each berry divides in four,
A kernel of knowledge
For each stage of the cycle.

Through tears of awareness,
I hang it on my door,
Grateful for bittersweet lessons
Reminders of the autumn of life.

November 21, 1998

This is the Season

This is the season for long reflective walks
     For roads not taken
     For things that might have been
     For remembering the way things were
     And will never be again.
This is the season for remembering
     Friends long gone
     Friends who are leaving
     And friends whose parting
     Is still a fresh wound on our hearts.
This is the season of radical changes
     In the weather
     In our lives
     As children grow
     Leaving us behind.
This is the season for letting go
     Facing new challenges
     Closing chapters
     Opening doors.

1992

Enter the Silence

Snow falls deep
In the old wood
Behind the barn

The wind can't reach
Trees
Cradled by hills

Thick white flakes
Gently land
On laden limbs
Muffling all sound

Under the rising moon
Long slender shadows
Tree shapes
Stretched and twisted
Paint black patterns
On the white bright snow

There I enter
The silence
Of my imagination.

December 1997

The Forgotten Smell of Snow

Along a Wisconsin river sat three crows big as ravens,
feathers puffed against the cold.
Squatting down to protect their feet,
they faced the winter wind.
Bright black eyes regarded me suspiciously,
reluctant to fly unless there was need.
To give them security,
I pretended not to see,
and taking a deep breath, discovered
the forgotten smell of snow.

March 1996

The Hawk Blew in from Chicago Last Night

The Hawk blew in from Chicago last night
Coating the west side of trees with white
The woods became a stand of Birch in the misty morning.

The Hawk blew in from Chicago last night
And stayed all day
Tugging at hats and making eyes water.

The Hawk blew in from Chicago last night
Filling the silence of the woods along the Mohawk
With its sharp cry.

The Hawk blew in from Chicago last night
I seemed to hear it howl,
"You can run, but cannot hide."

November 23, 2002
After moving East from Chicago

Primal Solstice

Electric pools of artificial light
bathe the people in islands of brightness
against the blacktop of the parking lot.
Their isolation stark as stars in a winter sky.
Internal timepieces as old as memory
send them scurrying about their tasks,
anxious to return to hearth and home.

The growing darkness triggers ancient behaviors
in a people removed from the cycles of season.
With all the insulating modern convenience
of car, computer, lights, TV,
they cannot escape.
Their response to fading sunlight is primal,
instinctive, and preserving,
as is their desire for human warmth.

December 1997

Nature & Spirituality

Prairie Smoke

Out of the mists of my mind
An Old One wrapped in a blanket
Ascends the hill.

Older than time,
A face beyond age and wisdom,
I know him by the clothes he wears.

The grey-brown blanket around his shoulders
Offers him small comfort.
He coughs and pulls it close.

Breathing heavily, he struggles upward.
At his waist, a digging stick and a small pouch
Identify his task.

Slowly he makes his way to the summit.
I watch as he takes a pinch of tobacco from the pouch.
Singing, he offers it to the directions.

He kneels before the small plant I had been studying.
Our offerings of tobacco intertwine the physical and spirit worlds.
He gives thanks, digs a small root, and descends as the vision fades.

Before me, Prairie Smoke's bright red bombs
hang from delicate stalks
Then burst in upright flames and filaments of smoke
A testament to the fire that keeps this fen alive

February 3, 2004

Trees

Each tree has its place
To strengthen and to heal
To give comfort to those seeking shelter
To grow with others until
Together
In peace and harmony
They become a sacred forest
That shows us how to live.

The forest is stronger
If the trees are varied:
Elm, Sycamore, Pine
Ash, Maple, Oak, Cedar.
Each has a gift to bring.
Each has a strength.
Some are resistant to fire,
Some to disease.
If one falls, there is another
to take its place.

So are we stronger
If our community
Has many voices.
Each raised in praise
And thanksgiving
In its own way.
Each voice heard
Until a melody becomes harmony
And harmony becomes a symphony.
A symphony of voices,
Each voice playing a part
Pleasing to the ear and
All of Creation.

August 1996

We Give Thanks for the Gift of Trees

We give thanks for
The sweetness of Apple, Pear, and Cherry.
They grace the spring with delicate blossoms of white and pink
And satisfy our bellies with wholesome fruit in autumn.

We give thanks for
The strength of Oak.
Its branches gracefully reach for the Earth.
It shelters all within its circle round.
Its acorns sustain our Brothers and Sisters throughout the winter.

We give thanks for
The gentle Maple
Which releases the sweet sap of spring
To cleanse the bitter taste of winter from our mouths and hearts.
Its leaves blaze forth in golds and reds
Glorifying the blue skies of autumn.

We give thanks for
The supple grace of Willow.
Its branches give shape to our baskets.
Its bark gives the medicine that eases pain in our joints
And fever in our brows.

We give thanks for
The upright elegance of Elm.
With lifted arms, it carries our prayers skyward.
In the cathedral presence of its branches
We speak our hearts.

We give thanks for
The comfort of Cottonwood.
Its fluffy seeds float lazily along
The warm currents of late spring air
Reminding us to slow down and enjoy the days.
Friendly Poplar leaves wave in summer breezes.
Rustling, their voices call for gentle rains.

We give thanks for
The fresh scent of Pine.
Its needles bring sweet dreams.
Peace resides in soft, snow-covered branches
Which shelter birds and animals from the cold.
The nuts in its cones provide nourishment
As welcome as its promise of green growing on a wintry evening.

October 1997

In Praise of Caterpillars

Let go of expectations.
Enjoy the moment.
Savor each leaf.
Revel in the warmth of the sun
The cool of the shade
The refreshing dew.

Be the very best
Caterpillar you can be.
Time enough to retreat
To the inner world.
To become a butterfly
Is inevitable.

October 2000

Vines

Tiny tendrils reach
stretching, yearning
for something~anything
to hold onto…
In innocence they grasp
what first they touch.
Their sensitive tips twine tightly,
a lifeline in their search.
Is it true?
Will it hold?
Or false security
that gives way
when needed most?
Hope sends out a second probe
no less desperate than the first
to secure success.

Life is like a vine.
To grow, one must reach out
Touch and cling to the unproven.
Faith and trust combine
with sheer will to climb.
To reach the heavens
One must risk a fall.

June 29, 1997

The Magic of the Night Blooming Gourd Plants

In the deep darkness,
A light from the back of the house
Illuminates the yard
Casting deep, dark shadows
Among the elephant ear leaves of the gourd vines
Growing behind the garage.

The warm night air hangs heavy
With the pungent smell of the sweating plants.
Their ruffly white flowers glow luminescent in the weak light.
Overhead the leaves of trees rustle in the wind
Speaking of the approaching storm, still miles away.

I walk among the vines that canopy the garden
Encouraging them to be strong
Whispering to the fuzzy baby gourds
"Hang on, grow big."
Shoots of new growth reach out over the path,
Demanding attention and support.
I pet the furry big leaves,
Caressing them between my palms, loving their softness.
I can feel the hunger of the plants,
Like the hunger of a woman in the late stages of pregnancy,
As their roots seek nourishment and water from the rich soil of
        the Earth.
Strong tendrils, like fingers and hands, seek support to pull
        themselves up
As their heavy, pregnant wombs fight to give birth to new life.

At the same time there is sensuality
In the blooming male and female flowers in the autumn night.
I can smell their musk in the heat and humidity.

There is a rich depth to their sexuality that wasn't there earlier in
        the season.
It speaks of their maturity and awareness of all of life's stages.
I dip my finger into the male flower
I feel the feathery dryness of the pollen.
Carefully I carry it over to a female flower six inches away.
By contrast, the female receptors are swollen and aroused.
I gently rub my finger against them.
They grow moist with my touch, and slippery.

On the other side of the fence are more female flowers.
A few males poke their heads out
Through the fence for their one night's bloom.
I repeat the process, picking up the pollen dust on my fingertip
I spread it against the hard pistils of the female flowers.
They grow wet with the stimulation.
Each time I marvel at the experience of union, conception, and birth.
Magic is in the night.

September 1997

The Rock, The River, The Tree

I have heard the Rock People speak
With voices so loud and deep
My body vibrated with the sound.

I have heard the Rocks sing
And my soul answered their song
With one of my own.

I have heard the Tree People call my name
And tell me their stories
In pictures and poetry beyond the reach of words.

I have listened to the River
Rushing down from glacier-capped mountains
And been in awe of the sound of ancient voices
Joyous in fresh found freedom.

The Rock, the River, the Tree
All talk to me
When I listen and am still.

June 1996

Music Resounds

Music resounds
In the Earth.
The Earth is alive
With the sound.

Music resides
In the Earth.
Music Resides
In me.

It vibrates my soul,
My body responds,
Touching my mind:
Remember! Awaken! Live! Breathe!

The beat of the Earth
Is the bass note of life.
The beat of the Earth
Is the base.

The rhythms of Earth
Beat in my heart.
The rhythms of Earth
Beat in yours.

Hear them!
Listen!
Connect!
Rejoice!

The sounds of the Earth
Are ground for my roots.
The sounds of the Earth
Lift my wings.

The song of the Earth,
Voices like thunder,
The song of the Earth
Vibrates my dreams.

Music resounds
In the Earth.
The Earth is alive
With the sound.

July 1997

Release

Release
Let it go
Accept that which is
Lose the world and
Gain your soul

October 2000

Soon

Soon it is coming
feel the pulsing drum
the beat awakens
the heart
beats in rhythm
anticipation

Soon it is coming
the pulse quickens
you're more alive
headlong you rush
into the abyss

you know not what
awaits, but
soon it is coming
destiny or destruction
soon

December 1997

The Dragons of the Waters of Life

Way down deep
in the bottom of the lake
lies the dragon.
Waiting. Watching.

One eye open
the other eye closed
ever vigilant
biding his time.

Blue are the depths
and black the mud
at the bottom
of the Lake of the Waters of Life.

In the Cave of the Moon
his sister sleeps.
The tides rise and fall
with her every breath.

She draws waters in
and the tides retreat.
She releases the waves
and the tides rush to shore.

The Waters of Life have a rhythm
controlled by the Dragon of the Moon.
Slowly. Evenly.
In and out.

Our bodies feel the tug
of the dragon's breath,
as she sleeps and dreams
in the Cave of the Moon.
The dragons are Guardians
protecting the flow
Keep them safe.
Keep them pure.

Brother and sister
together they work
to bring harmony
to the Waters of Life.

June 1996

Mayan Moon

From my cave I awaken at sunset
to fly forth on the wings of night.
I spill my magic over hills and valleys.
Rivers and lakes reflect my light.

Those who seek me are touched by beauty.
The muse is strong when they call my name.
But my cup flows with love and madness;
Those who dwell with me are not the sane.

Ocean waters pull to reach me.
Seeds spring forth when my face is full
But my radiance begins to dwindle
as from my cup it freely spills.

Then I retreat to my cave of darkness
to sleep, to renew, to fill up again.
Then I can fly in all my splendor.
The cycle repeats: I wax; I wane.

September 1994

The Ronora Poems

Camp Ronora in Watervliet, Michigan is a magical place where beauty soothes
the senses. These three poems and "The Four Sacred Plant Mothers Came" were
inspired by experiences there.

Awakening Sky

Mist rises from the meadow grasses in the early morning.
Birds sit on wires in prayerful stillness awaiting the sun.
A graceful dance of silent women greets the dawn in moving
        meditation
Under the ever changing colors of the awakening sky.

Blue Heron

A rainbow spray blows over the water
As iridescent dragonflies flit among the cattails and water lilies.
Across the lake a Blue Heron is not afraid to stick its neck out
To take a step forward.

Seven Swans at Sunset

Rippling waves like tiny mirrors reflect the golden light.
Bare, black tree branches stand in bas-relief against the bright.
Overhead seven swans circle the water in flight.
Two land in the lake as the sun says, "goodnight".

April 1996

The Four Sacred Plant Mothers Came
(To be recited accompanied by a heartbeat rhythm on a drum)

Around a fire a circle of women
Stood in the meadow, bathed in the light.
Their voices were chanting; their drums beat a heartbeat.
At their feet, candles glowed in the night.
Slowly, majestically, masked beings entered
Each one a spirit of a sacred plant.
Corn Mother, Bean Mother, Squash Mother entered,
Carrying their bounty in baskets in hand.

These three are Sisters sent to sustain us.
Both fresh and dried, they ease winter's pain.
Starflower-Strawberry, blood red and juicy,
Strawberry, Queen of the Plants also came.

Overhead stars shone. Rain clouds had parted.
Overhead moon glow lighted their way.
Out of the woodlands, the spirits came walking.
To talk to the women, to each have her say.

Strawberry speaks in the East, facing westward.
Opposite her, the Bean Mother talks.
Integrity, dignity, each one possessing,
A map for the Earth Path, each of us walks.

Corn is our roots, in the South, our stability.
Her Truth travels northward where wisdom resides
In Squash Mother, who shares her ability
To learn of survival in uncertain tides.

I wish you had been there. I wish you had seen them.
The night was enchanted, the women the same.
Corn Mother, Bean Mother, Squash Mother, Strawberry,
The Four Sacred Plant Mothers, all of them came.

Strawberry's face glowed pink in the darkness
She spoke of the magic of each woman's blood
And how like the moon, each of us cleanses
The importance of keeping ourselves pure in spring's mud.

Corn Mother's kernels were many in color.
Golden tassels of Truth streamed from her face.
Corn gives us humor, our strength in Earth changes.
Corn brings fertility to each human race.

Beans sometimes test one's sense of one's dignity.
But Bean Mother always nurtures her own.
Beans and their magic call Grandfather West Winds,
Beans bring the rains that make all green things grow.

The coppery visage of Squash Mother smiled sweetly.
Her fruit looks like women, and sometimes like men.
She spoke of the magic when two fit so neatly.
She spoke of the Mystery as one born again.

I wish you had been there. I wish you had seen them.
The night was enchanted, the women the same.
Corn Mother, Bean Mother, Squash Mother, Strawberry,
The Four Sacred Plant Mothers, all of them came.

April 1996

Jupiter

This poem is based on a ceremony led by Grandmother Twylah Nitsch at the Seneca Wolf Clan Teaching Lodge on the Cattaraugus Reservation in Brant, New York. It was held in the summer of 1994 just as two asteroids hit Jupiter. During the ceremony a diamond shape appeared before all of us on the earthen floor of the lodge, it expanded into a small circle, about eighteen inches in diameter, and revealed events, much like television. Many of us were transfixed by what we saw before our own eyes. The magic was greatly enhanced when several days later we left the reservation and saw the color photographs that NASA put out. In traditional mythology, Jupiter is the planet of abundance.

The sunlight formed a pattern upon the earthen floor
The sunlight made a diamond shape where it never shone before.
The diamond was a window into a different world,
It changed into a circle and we watched as scenes unfurled.
A circle streaked with darker lines drawn across its face
Two explosions near darker spots within that windowed space.

The teaching lodge was dark that day with timber roof and beams.
The women talked of portents that had come into their dreams.
They'd seen the shape of diamond, they knew what it must mean.
The magic of the moment, when they knew what they had seen.
But stunned they were to see it there upon the earthen floor,
And stunned to see the sunlight, where it never shone before.
At the feet of Twylah, who talked of prophecy,
Jupiter, the planet, took the hits for you and me.
And as she spoke we watched the scene, we were simply mesmerized
To know that Earth was in the path of comets twice that size.

The air was still. The people too in prayerful stillness stood.
Families with children, who were very, very good.
The Fourth World soon is ending, Harmony will reign
But with endings there is sadness, fear of sorrow and of pain.
I was glad I was saw the portent as it appeared within that space.
I was glad for the community that gathered in that place.
I knew that they'd be with me, and I would be with them

Whenever things start happening, I can count upon my clan.
We face the future, knowing that survival's ours to gain
And that courage, faith and wisdom are the tools to build again.

April 1996

Code of Creeping Charlie:
The Rhyme of the Fool

Ode from Glechoma hederacea in the Lamiaceae, commonly called Creeping
Charlie, Mouse Ears, Ground Ivy, Gill-Over-The-Ground, and ruder things.

Out! Out! Out! I say!
I make the others back away!
I need more space to dance and play!

Some think me Wise. Some think me Fool.
But I know what I need to do:
I'll make you laugh. I'll break all rules.

Fences are for other folks.
There are no boundaries; they're only jokes.
The summer's short. No time to waste.
And so I'm always in your face.

But should you ever need a friend,
My tender heart is yours to bend.
But careful please cause it will break,
If you should leave me in your wake.

2002

Women & Spirituality

A Circle of Women

We welcome the Spirit of the Young Girl-Child
May she grow in innocence and love
Learning to trust her place in the world
As she is nurtured by our love and understanding.

We welcome the Spirit of the Young Woman
In all her beauty and grace
May she experience the strength of her emotions
And discover the ways she is unique in all of creation.

We welcome the Spirit of the Woman Full Grown
We celebrate her creativity and love of other
As she expands the self by giving birth
Nurturing ideas, life, community, and art.

We welcome the Spirit of the Wise Woman
She who sees clearly the patterns of life
Who has the wisdom to interpret them
And the grace to let others learn for themselves.

We welcome the Spirits of the Women Who have Come Before
Through which we connect with the Web of all Life
Receiving inspiration and guidance all our lives
Until we join them to help those still Earthly bound.

We welcome the Spirits of the Women Yet to Come
Knowing that it is on Earth we receive the strongest lessons
We seek to stretch our minds, bodies, and spirits
As we gather together and prepare for Your future.

We welcome the Spirit of our Inner Knowing
That spark of divine that connects us one to another
Mother to daughter, sister to sister, friend to friend
We seek to expand our circle, embracing All.

Written as an invocation for WomanSpirit 1995

The Weaver

I weave the cloth of women.
Their stories and their lives
pass through my warp
as the weft from my shuttle
sings across the loom.

I weave the cloth of women:
I thread the heddles,
sley the reed.
Unfold the colors!
Unfold the dreams!

The beater beats the heartbeat
Of the rhythm of the loom.
The harness lifts,
The shuttle flies,
The pattern winds upon the beam.

Pedals fall and heddles rise:
Tunnels of colors,
the weft of their lives.
Their souls in every pass
of the continuous thread.

Unfold the textures!
Release the songs!
Wonder at intricacies revealed!
I weave the cloth of women
Their stories and their lives.

December 1996

We are the Weavers of Wisdom

We are the weavers of wisdom:
Pass it on.   Pass it on.
From our mothers to our daughters
Pass it on.   Pass it on.
Generation to generation
Pass it on.   Pass it on.
Sister to sister, friend to friend.
Pass it on.   Pass it on.

Our Spirit asks the questions.
Pass it on.   Pass it on.
Our hearts hold the answers.
Pass it on.   Pass it on.
Our Minds find the way.
Pass it on.   Pass it on.
Our hands make it happen.
Pass it on.   Pass it on.

From our bodies children come.
Pass it on.   Pass it on.
From our love they learn and grow.
Pass it on.   Pass it on.
Working for a better world,
Pass it on.   Pass it on.
We are the weavers of wisdom.
Pass it on.   Pass it on.
Pass it on.   Pass it on.

April 1990

Wildflowers

Wildflowers gaily grace the grasses
Giving color to the green of life.
Each of them supports the other
Standing proud, roots entwined.
Their colors do not blend but shout,
"I'm Blue!   I'm Yellow!   I'm Red! "
And when the season passes
Their deeds give promise
To the next generation.

My Wildflowers

Each of these poems is about a woman friend. Each gives strength to the other.

Diana Flower Garden
Eyes of China Blue
Sees a woman twice her age
Reflected in her mirror.

Marilla's sweet heart
Dissolves in tears:
So many worlds to travel
So little time.

Regal Elise, tall and proud
Her pioneer spirit forges onward
New things to do
New worlds to conquer!

Little Bertha, once so strong
Afraid to be alone
Bravely walks through life
Now filled with blues and blacks.

Moondancer shines
Reflecting light
As laughter skips
Across the water.

Gentle Violet
Whose soft voice speaks
Worlds of wisdom.
Will no one hear?

Carol retreats and Little Ones,
Rosie and the rest,
Come out to play
While alter Tom protects.

Katie bright
Katie did
Katie right
Katie does again.

Regal Karen
Upright and proud
Rides life's bumpy road
Armed with bluster.

Ya-Weh-Node's black eyes sparkle
Ya-Weh-Node's black eyes snap
Her black eyes see your soul
While Crystal Lights shine.

July 1996

Salt Creek in Sundance Valley

a hot summers day
a cool flowing creek
a circle of women
skirts lifted
wade in water
or sit on the bank
comforting one who cries

sunlight filters through trees
dappled patterns fall from skies
gentling gentle faces
one fills a water bag
one wears a straw hat
outside the circle
a small child plays quietly

softly they chant
harmonies form naturally
patterns shift but remain the same
women gather on a hot day
escaping for a moment
responsibilities
patterns shift but remain the same
women gather for thousands of years.

July 31, 1997

Prayers of Everyday Life

The next three poems were inspired by my good friend and mentor, the Rev. Ed Searl. Ed called me one day as I lay abed with pneumonia and reminded me that I was congregational reader for the upcoming Sunday. Normally Ed provides the readings, but he said that his topic was Wabi, the art of imperfection, and he was having trouble finding something appropriate and suggested I write a piece. I told him that I really wasn't up to it, but when I couldn't find anything either, I came up with these. Ed included the first one in his book, *A Place of Your Own*, published by Berkley Books, New York.

In Praise of Imperfection
An Ode to Middle Age

My daughter stands before the mirror
Cheeks sucked in
Mouth pursed in a bow
Arranging a wayward lock.
"I hate my hair!" she exclaims.
I sigh.
Imperfection is so much easier
When you do not have a choice.
That's why I love middle age.

When I was young I worried about:
My weight
My hair
Shape
My derriere.
Now I buy a larger size.

Youth is a time of competition.
The subtle comparison at the beach:
The size of breasts
The muscle tone
The tan, the grace
The curve of hips.
Now I think, "Not bad for an old broad!'

And dig into potato chips.
It's much more fun being middle aged.

There's a comfort that comes from the well worn and familiar,
Be it shoes or body or relationships.
When there's love and lovely shared experiences,
Flaws become endearments.
Whether scars, jokes, or scuffs,
It's much easier being middle aged.
The shift I find is one of attitude,
Of acceptance and love for myself and others,
Our bodies are there to keep us human.
Imperfection is a fact of life,
Something that marks us unique, not factory-made,
A living, breathing part of creation,
All be it of middle age.

April 1996

The Soul of Wabi

My house is filled with beautiful things
that have seen better days.
Antique clocks that don't keep time,
And chime when the spirit strikes them.

The Empire sofa is hard and straight
with filigree that isn't quite all there.
Tarnished gilt. Wavy mirrors.
Remembrances with lovely lines.

And yet I wouldn't trade them
in their faded glory
for newer, perfect things
that have no soul.

April 1996

Shards of Memory

Shards of my grandmother's china
Grace my garden gaily.
Their gilded edges twinkle in the sun.
Their painted flowers blossom in the snow.

I do not throw them out,
But gift the spirits gladly
In the manner of the Ancient Ones
Across the great Southwest.

Eccentric my neighbors think~and worse
But I don't care. I know
That Fairies dine upon them~and Sprites
In the magic of Midsummer's Eve.

April 1996

I do not want to save the world today

I do not want to save the world today.
The air is warm and moist with melting snow.
The sun is bright and high in the sky.
The crocus pop through the earth.

I do not want to save the world today.
My grandson is born this morning.
Mom and Babe are well.
New life beckons and I want to play.

I do not want to save the world today.
I do not want to write and copy, sort and mail.
I'm very tired and want to sleep but
How can I miss one moment?

I do not want to save the world today.
I'll save the world tomorrow.

February 22, 2000

Grandma Memories

I hear the sounds of my grandson
Playing in his bed
Happy sounds of a contented child.

I know I should wait.
Let him enjoy
His private morning moments,
But temptation is too great
And our time together too brief.

Gently I push the door open.
I'm greeted by a glorious grin.
A bouncing boy cooing, "Hi!"
Grateful to be released from behind bars
He gives great hugs.

Safe in Grandma's arms
He travels down wooden stairs
To roughhouse on Grandma's bed.
We play, we laugh.
Squeals and giggles all around.
Unconditional love is the best breakfast.

October 2000

Stepping Off the Rainbow

I've always wondered,
Why race to find the end
When the view from the rainbow top
Must be so glorious?

Pots of gold have never interested me.
A journey through the colors fascinates me.
Seeing the world through rainbow hues,
The purity of seven, the wonder of thirteen,
And the infinite blend of possibilities.

Is the Road to Ithaca paved with rainbows?
I think so. But how wide is a rainbow?
And won't that first step off be exhilarating!
Looking back to see the pattern of the whole,
I wonder if my rainbow will have a companion
Or will there be thousands of dancing rainbow lights?

April 26, 2000

Defying Gravity is Good for the Soul

How I love flying!
The race down the runway
The expansion of the chest on takeoff
The adrenaline rush of the upward thrust
The lift that sends me soaring
The release of responsibility
The freedom of the sky
Defying gravity is good for the soul!
Finally, the satisfaction of a gentle touchdown
Feet back on the ground, life intrudes again.

October 2000

Friends & Relationships

The Two Are One

for Mary & Alex in honor of their wedding June 26, 1993

As shadows shape the things we see,
To know the light,
We must experience the dark.
The two are one.

Discord makes sweeter harmony
The highs defined
By lows in life and song.
The two are one.

Textures and patterns intertwine
Future and past
Follow as night and day.
The two are one.

One voice cannot sing harmony,
But one and one
Combine to make a blend.
And two are one.

Your voice then compliments my own
Giving mine shape
In pitch and tone. Together we
Become as one.

This poem was beautifully put to music by Chris Garofalo and sung by our son,
Rick.

Joe

Walking down the street
I saw you half a block ahead.
My heart and pace quickened
For just a moment.

Your name was on my lips
As I thought, "Wait up!"
Then I remembered
You are gone.

This man was so like you
Your height, your build
Your hair, your walk.
I miss you, Joe.

You are with me still
So close and yet so far
Not of this Earth, but
A breath away.

I stood and watched him
Catch the light
And hurry on ahead
Leaving me behind.

See you soon, old friend.

2002

She Who Follows

Names are very revealing and have several interpretations, often showing positive and negative. When my friend, Glenda, a leader if there ever was one, received her name from Grandmother Twylah, she was horrified to learn that the translation meant, "She Who Follows". I wrote this for her but it is true of many strong women.

"I'm Not!"
You cried silently to yourself.
But I heard.
"There must be some mistake.
I'm a leader."

"Of course you are,"
I wanted to reply.
"But you follow too."

Follow your heart.
Follow your dreams.
Follow your vision.
Follow your truth.

But as with all names
There is another meaning.
You are She Who Comes After.

You follow in the footsteps
Of women who dare:

Dare to challenge.
Dare to find a new way.
Dare to be different.
Dare to lead.
And look at the legions behind you.

The Gift of Roots and Wings

For my friend and mentor, Oak and Druid, the Rev. Ed Searl, who has provided a
spiritual home for so many.

A steady oak stands tall, roots deep and fast in prairie earth.
Open branches welcome all under sheltering canopy.
Bark all gnarly and twisted, trunk strong and straight,
This gentle oak, this fair oak,
This steady oak stands tall above the rest.

In its branches rests a nest cradling precious eggs.
Each one lovingly tended by a tender parent
Till one by one they hatch.
Tirelessly each chick is nurtured, given just what it needs
To grow in wisdom and the ways of its kind.
Summer breezes rock the nest,
Storms and rains threaten its safety,
But inhabitants are doubly protected
By parent and tree working together.

Soon the time comes when birds must fly
To find their own way in the world.
Fledglings test their wings, confident in lessons well received.
Opportunities provided.
Reluctant to leave their shelter,
The lure of open sky beckons
They take the plunge.

Under their wings, the air supports them.
But what really keeps them aloft
Is the support of parent and tree when they needed them most.
Each summer season brings a new set of eggs to the nest
And the cycle repeats:
The gift of roots and wings by those who care.

November 1997

A Heart Too Well Protected

Within her tower of stone
a beautiful woman sat alone
in the dark.
Sadness shadows crossed her face
and permeated the gloom.
Shivering and cold,
she stared into the vast expanse
of a deep dark well.
Through its mirror she saw life reflected.
She waited, but it passed her by.

All around her towers grew brambles,
thick with thorns.
Its strong oak door was swollen shut
and barred, but no one mourned.
Her guardian, to protect her,
had kept the world at bay.
And no one came to visit.
And no one came to stay.

Finally a small plant grew
among the damp grey stones.
Its cinnamon scent
awoke in her a memory:
She had flown!
A yearning grew inside of her
to be flying on the wind
free and fearless taking wing---
Flying once again.

The spark of faith flickered and flamed.
The breath of love gave life.
The warming glow dispelled the pain,

the suffering and the strife.
Suddenly slanting sunlight streamed
across the stone-cold floor.
She called her Guardian to the gate,
"Open wide the oaken door
and tame the brambles round
so they can bloom once more."

Now, covered in roses,
Stands a cottage once castle wall.
Morning Glories scent the air
in gardens green and tall.
Tended by a tender woman,
it is a welcoming place
and all who come are touched
by her simple, caring grace.
For a heart too well protected,
languishes alone.
But a heart that's warm and open
builds a refuge all call home.

April 1996

That Love May Grow

That I may hear your words
Listen to mine.
That I may know your heart,
Speak to mine.
That I may follow your dreams,
Share mine.
That I may grow in love,
Grow with mine.
That I may share your life,
Give me time.

April 1996

Thirty-Three Years

You are so far away
I have to shout to be heard
But I can't breathe
Because there isn't any air.

When did you stop loving me, I cry
I do love you, you reply
Then when did I stop
Being able to feel your love.

The shortest distance between two points
Is a straight line
If both are facing
One another.

Please turn around
And so will I.

August 1998

The Promise of the Stone

I found an amazing stone on Jupiter Island. It appeared to be two figures intertwined. I wondered about it and that night dreamed this dream.

Separated by miles,
Two souls sleep.
Seeking communion,
Their Spirits rise.
Glowing ghostly blue-white,
They journey.
High above the earthly plane,
They search.
Reaching one another,
They entwine.
Loving beyond all reason,
They become as one.
Unwilling to separate,
They cling.
Turning to stone,
They fall to Earth.
To be found on the beach,
Given as a promise.

December 1997

Don't Touch!

Don't touch!
Or if you do,
Be gentle.
My rough thick bark
Has been stripped away
And I am as tender
As a new-born babe:
A cut would fester, scab and scar.
A bruise would bleed and blacken.

Take care!
This smooth, thin membrane
Is very fine.
A soft caress would feel so sweet,
But an unkind word would scratch and mar
This delicate veneer.
Oil would be very soothing,
And protect my new-found openness.
Treated right, I may develop a patina
Glorious and glowing,
Lustrous as a precious pearl,
For you alone.

April 1996

Lying Alone

Lying alone
I think of you
Missing your touch
The caress of your eyes

In my mind
You are with me
I can almost smell
Your sweet skin

Feel the weight
Of your body
Next to mine
In the dark

A warm flush
Surrounds me
The ache dims
But not the yearning

Awakened now
And lying alone

1998

Touch Me

Touch is an art
That gets better with practice
Isolation leads to alienation
And you lose your touch

Life without touch
Has no art
Life without art
Has no meaning

Touch me
So I can breathe
Touch me
So I can feel
Touch me
So I can cry
Touch me
So I can live again
Touch me.

1996

Sea Song

My body holds the waters of life
Salty and fresh my spray
My soul is wide and deep as the deepest sea

Moving, ever moving
Flowing, ever flowing
I respond to the rhythms of the tides
I undulate as the waves roll to shore

I feel the power within me
Coming from the darkest night
Riding, riding
Riding the crest
Holding my breath
As it breaks the surface
Then gasping for air
I lay back and enjoy the rush
Then wait for the next set
To carry me along

July 1997

Benedictions

September 11, 2001

Let us pray...
For all who lost their lives
For all who lost their loved ones
For all who are hurt and suffering
For all who are providing aid
For all who are missing
For all who do not know where their loved ones are
For all who are haunted by the sounds and images
For all who were led to do this deed
For all who must now go forward and lead the way
May they have wisdom, strength, courage, and love.

Oh, South Africa

Robbin Island, once a Leper Colony, then the prison that held Nelson Mandela, is now a museum to South Africa's struggle against Apartheid. All who visit are profoundly moved by the experience. I had the privilege of carrying an African flag as those attending the Parliament of the World's Religions in Cape Town planted a Peace Pole on the site.

Where the heat of the Indian Ocean
Meets the cold of the Atlantic,
Africa dips her toe.

Pouring off the continent in a tablecloth of mist
All the pain and suffering drain
In Earth's healing waters
And wholeness is born in rich diversity.

The sun rises in one world
Bears witness to South Africa
And sets in another.

December 2, 1999

Go In Peace

Dedicated to Marilla Thurston Missbach December 3, 1996

It is not death I fear but dying,
That long, slow decline of body and mind
trapping the essence that is me within.
How lucky those that do not linger,
but finish up their work quickly and are gone.

I am not brave.
I do not want to watch my friends and loved ones travel onward,
leaving me behind to mourn not their passing, but my loss.
I am not brave.
I fear pain and suffering even more
and the numbing, dumbing effect of drugs most.

Yet, how wonderful to see the garden that is my life
Pass through its seasons—all of them.
Savoring each one fully and denying none.

The springtime planning and plowing
Knowing that the seeds that I and others planted are
Drinking in the rain, gaining nourishment from the rich earth
Receiving inspiration from the warming sun.
Growing, ever growing, throughout the summer.

Protecting my garden from those things that would destroy it.
Weeding out the things that are not needed.
Replanting with new ideas and experiences.
Finally, giving up my bounty for the benefit of others.
The joy of sharing, of loving,
Knowing that as I am consumed, I become one with
   the Universe.

That is the time to go
Not the time of bud,
Not the time of full-flower
But the time of joyful letting go.

And yet, there comes a time when the field is at rest, that fallow
        time,
When one reflects upon the circle of the seasons of life
And sees with clear eye what has been done, and what has been
        left undone.
Perhaps after all, that winter is the time of letting go.
If that is so, let me go in grace
With a contented heart that comforts those I leave behind.
Let my mind be strong, my spirit pure,
        and my life inspire those who are touched by it.
Then will I go in peace.

December 1995

Published by the
Ice Cube Press
est. 1993

this book is printed on acid-free, recycled paper
& uses Tempus Sans (ITC)

The cover photos were taken
by Melinda Morris Perrin.

Printer Device by Andrew Driscoll

find other books of interest
on our web site catalog
www.icecubepress.com

For twenty-one years, Melinda Morris Perrin lived as a Mid-westerner, working as a television producer for much of that time. During that period she studied with many Native American teachers and became a teacher of the Seneca Wolf Clan Teaching Lodge and the Seneca Indian Historical Society. A Plant Spirit Medicine practitioner, Ms. Perrin has been a leader and spiritual healer of the Prairyerth UU Fellowship since 1998. She was a presenter at the Parliament of the World's Religions in Cape Town, South Africa, the keynote speaker at the University of Iowa's Fall Colloquium's, Harvest Lecture: "Natural Prayers" and is a frequent presenter and guest lecturer at universities and Unitarian Universalist congregations throughout the United States. She was co-chair of the PrairyErth Living Treasures of North America Heritage Awards for four years. Ms. Perrin earned triple honors in her degree program in Natural Religion, Earth Law, & Ethnobotany at Northeastern Illinois University in 2002. She was the Executive Director of the Conservation Research Institute when she and her husband, Dan, moved back to New York in 2002. Her poetry is included in *A Place of Your Own* by Edward Searl and she is a frequent contributor to *Sophia*, a quarterly publication of Women & Religion, and *Whirling Rainbow*. She is the proud mother of Alex, Rick, and Jessica, and a doting grandmother. This is her first book.